Adopting Alfred

A story about adoption from a birth child's perspective

By Emma Lovelace

Illustrated by Olha Pankiv

My name is Alice and I am 10 years old.
I live at home with my mummy and daddy, just the three of us and I love it!
My mummy and daddy do so much with me...

All of my friends at school have brothers and sisters.
I've never had a brother or sister before!
That was until....

One afternoon when mummy and daddy asked me if I would like a little brother or sister!
I'd wanted a sibling for a long long time!!

I asked mummy, "Do you have a baby growing in your tummy?"
Mummy said, "no, but there are other ways to have a brother or a sister Alice".

Mummy said one way was called 'adoption'.
I'd heard about this before, there was a boy in my class who was adopted.

Adoption means a family gives a child a home to keep them safe and loved...just like I am!
If a child is adopted it means they can't stay with their birth parents.

Birth parents are the child's other parents. The mummy grows the baby in her tummy like all the other mummies do but the birth mummy and daddy cannot look after the baby.

I didn't know whether my mummy and daddy would adopt a boy or girl. What would they be like I wondered!? How old would they be? Would they like the same things as me?
Mummy and daddy explained that adopting would take a long time and that Debbie the social worker would help us.

A social worker is a person who helps all the children find a family.
I talked to Debbie a lot! Sometimes with mummy and daddy, other times it was just Debbie and me.
Debbie asked me lots of questions like what do I enjoy doing? What do I like to eat? Her job is to get to know us all really really well.

One day after school mummy and daddy asked if they could show me a picture of a little baby boy. His name was Alfred and he needed a family!

I couldn't believe how cute and little he was. I wanted him to be my baby brother!
But we had to wait, even though I wanted to bring him home that day. He was all I could think about and I knew I'd be a great big sister to him.

When mummy and daddy said that baby Alfred was going to be a part of our family and that I would be meeting him soon I was so happy!!
I had been so excited...but then suddenly I felt a bit wobbly. I turned to mummy and asked, "will you still love me the same?"

I was suddenly worried that if I had a brother or sister that mummy and daddy might not love me as much anymore.
Mummy hugged me and said they would still love me just the same!

After that there were suddenly lots of visits to see Alfred at his foster carers house. A foster carer is a person who looks after the children until they find their new family.

I couldn't believe it when I finally met Alfred.
I'd been so excited on the journey over, but suddenly I felt shy.
I realised I didn't know what to do around baby Alfred.
I didn't know if he would like me, what toys he likes to play with or even how I would talk to him!

Mummy and daddy helped me and it made me feel much better.
After each visit I talked to mummy and daddy about my worries.

Then as the week went on my worries started to disappear and every morning I couldn't wait to see baby Alfred again.
The best bit was the day baby Alfred got to move into my house forever!!
I had helped daddy make his new bedroom all lovely and cosy.

I loved getting all of his toys out and helping with his bubble baths. I fed him his dinner using his spoon and made him giggle at games of 'peek-a-boo'.
Becoming a big sister was a bit of a change for me.

I had gone from having mummy and daddy all to myself and then all of a sudden I had to share them with baby Alfred.
But do you know what......

It was the best thing ever having baby Alfred as my little brother!!!
It doesn't matter that we didn't come from the same tummy.
All that matters is......

I love Alfred and Alfred loves me.

Printed in Great Britain
by Amazon